Renzo Chiarelli

VERONA

*195 Colour Photos and
Map of the City*

BET
BONECHI EDIZIONI -IL TURISMO- - FIRENZE

INDEX

Exclusive Distributors for Verona:
Randazzo Edizioni Turistiche
Via Emilei, 22
37121 Verona
Phone: 045/8004040
Fax: 045/8036063

© Copyright by Bonechi Edizioni "Il Turismo" S.r.l.
Via dei Rustici, 5 · 50122 Firenze · Tel. (055) 239.82.24/25
Telefax (055) 216.366

Photos: Bonechi · Edizioni "Il Turismo S.r.l. Archives
Layout: Piero Bonechi
Project Coordinator: Barbara Bonechi
Typesetting: Leadercomp, Florence
Reproductions: RAF, Florence
Printing: Lito Terrazzi, Florence

ISBN 88-7204-098-1

Aerial view of the city.

VERONA "GATEWAY TO ITALY"

Verona, Urbs Nobilissima, *is one of the most beautiful and ancient of all Italian cities – one which is justly famous and beloved both in Italy itself, and indeed, throughout the whole world. Today Verona has about 270 thousand inhabitants, and in the whole district of Veneto it is second only to Venice in wealth and importance.*

Its climate and accessibility are ideal, and Verona is a vital rail and road junction on the main route connecting Italy to Central Europe. It is a flourishing industrial, commercial and agricultural centre of international importance and is the site of the annual International Agricultural Show *and the* International Exhibition of Agricultural Machinery *– just two of the city's large exhibitions which attract visitors from all over Europe. The city is important in other fields as well – it is the home of the Mondadori firm of publishers, famous the world over. While on the subject of commerce, mention*

must be made of its wines, fruit, and of its marble, all of which are exported to many countries. Because of its fortunate geographical position and its importance as a European city, Verona has been described as The Gateway to Italy. *To travellers approaching from the North there is another sense in which Verona can be thought of as the* Gateway to Italy. *It is the first city which clearly possesses the appearance, harmony, character, the tradition and beauty of Italy, giving, as it were, a foretaste of the fundamental characteristics of the country as a whole. Verona's undeniable beauty has been celebrated by many foreign visitors who, from the earliest times have continued to pay tribute to the town in poetry and prose. Its beauty is essentially two-fold. Firstly, it is rich in natural beauty with its river, its hills, the nearby Lake Garda, and its background of mountains. Secondly, there is the great architectural beauty of the city itself with its buildings and monuments. Verona*

Panorama of the city from the Roman Theatre; opposite page: *San Giorgio in Braida seen from the Roman Theatre.*

is also an important cultural centre. It is a university city, with faculties of Economics, Languages, Education and Medicine, and a city rich in museums and distinguished libraries. But it is not just as an academic city that Verona has found fame, it has also become one of the major tourist centres of Italy. This is not surprising since the city as a whole is outstanding in what it has to offer the tourist. The people of Verona are friendly and welcoming, and a great deal of trouble is taken to make sure that the visitor really enjoys his stay. There are for example, theatrical performances staged during the warmer months, which include operas in the Roman Arena and Shakespearean plays in the Roman Theatre. There are Concert and Drama Societies and a highly renowned Academy of Music (Conservatorio di Musica). Finally we come to the one tourist attraction which makes Verona absolutely unique – its reputation given to it by Shakespeare's play, of being the town of Romeo and Juliet.

This, then, is the city which we have set out briefly to describe, with its traditions, its fine buildings, its distinguished monuments.

NOTES ON THE HISTORY AND ART OF VERONA

The origins of Verona are lost in the mists of time; it is not even known how the city came by its name. All that can be said with certainty is that it was in prehistoric times that human beings first settled in the place where the city was later to rise. The date of the first Roman occupation is not known for sure, but by the Ist Cent. B.C. Verona was already an important Roman settlement and the ancient centre of the town preserves the outlines of the original Roman nucleus which was known as *Augusta Verona*. Most of the important Roman remains in the town date from the Ist Cent. B.C. The town centre, like all towns founded on Roman military camps is divided by the "cardus" and the "decumanus" – at right angles to each other-into four "quarters". In the number and quality of its Roman remains – the Amphitheatre, the Theatre, the arches, gates, and bridges etc. – Verona is second only to Rome itself. From very early days Verona's geographical position was a vital factor in the city's importance. Three of the most important Roman roads started from there – the Augusta, the Gallica, and the Postumia. The city's importance as a strategic centre, which was to last nearly a thousand years, was evident by the Late Empire. During this period, several decisive battles were fought in the neighbourhood of Verona, such as the battles of Claudius against the Germans in 368 A.D., Constantine against Maxentius in 312 A.D. and Stilicho against Alaric in 402 A.D. Even as early as the Roman period, Verona had already become a cultural centre and produced one of the greatest Latin poets: Q. Valerius Catullus.

In the Middle Ages, Verona was again the scene of important events. Theodoric stayed there, as did Alboin, the Longobard, who was murdered in Verona by his wife Rosamund. Later, Pepin, the son of Charlemagne, visited Verona as did, Berengarius who died there in 924 in tragic circumstances.

Emperor *Otto I* of Germany came to the city to rescue Adelaide of Burgundy, who was held prisoner in the area. Despite invasions and wars, however, Verona still remained loyal to its cultural heritage. The city was fortunate in coming under the influence of two noble churchmen – the great Bishop St. Zeno during the IVth Cent. and the kindly Archdeacon Pacifico in the IXth Cent. Under the latter, there flourished one of the most famous Academies of the period, the Schola Sacerdotum. The city developed its own distinctive style of art, and this, combined with the influence of the Carolingian and Ottonian style, enriched the city with Early Christian basilicas and Pre-Romanesque churches. At about this time also, the Palace of Theodoric was beginning to take shape on the banks of the River Adige.

During the troubled times of the early XIIth Cent., the Commune of Verona was formed. The city became deeply involved in the bitter wars which swept through the whole country. The greatest of these was the conflicts between the Papacy and the Empire. In addition there were many purely local wars between neighbouring cities. But in spite of these conflicts, Verona flourished, not only in trade, but also in the arts, and as a political centre. In 1164, under this first Council, the Alliance of Verona came into being. This united all the mainland cities of the Veneto against Barbarossa and was to lead to the subsequent League of Lombardy. In 1226, Verona became a possession of the tyrannical *Ezzelino da Romano*. Then in 1263, *Leonardino della Scala*, nicknamed *Mastino*, was voted lord of the city, and thus began the rule of the great Scala (or Scaliger) family. Mastino was succeeded by *Alberto*, who died in 1301, and after him came his sons *Bartolomeo, Alboino* and *Can Francesco*. In 1308, Can Francesco became lord of the city, under the name Cangrande I. During his rule, the dominance of the Scala family reached its most glorious peak, with the city extending its influence over nearly all mainland Veneto. Cangrande, using his powers as the ruler of Verona, made the city into an antipapal stronghold. Its court became a cultural refuge and artists and writers flocked there in great number. Dante himself, who had previously been the guest of Cangrande's brother Bartolomeo, dedicated the third section of the Divine Comedy to his friend and patron, Cangrande. The death of Cangrande in 1329 marked the beginning of Verona's decline, despite the influence of a succession of dis-

Recent excavations have brought to light the foundations of the ancient Roman Porta dei Leoni or "Lions' Gate".

tinguished rulers. One of them was Mastino II, under whose rule, the sway of the Scala family was extended to include Brescia, Parma and Lucca. There was also Cangrande II, who built Castelvecchio and the superb bridge next to it, and then came the ferocious Cansignorio. The other great Italian ruling families, particularly those of Venice and Florence, often formed alliances against the Scalas, as the Papacy did itself. The rule of the Scala family finally come to an end with the flight of *Antonio della Scala* in 1387, after which the city fell into the hands of *Gian Galeazzo Visconti*. In 1404, Verona was conquered by the Carraresi, a powerful family from Padua; in 1405 it became part of the Venetian state. Venice retained its control over the city for nearly four hundred years, except for a brief period from 1509 to 1517, when Maximilian of Austria conquered it. Although the Venetian influence gave the city-state of Verona a long period of relative peace and prosperity, any suggestion of independence or desire for autonomy was firmly suppressed. As a result, the spirit and atmosphere of the city suffered severely. Verona's greatest artistic and cultural achievements came during the three centuries when the Town Council and the Scala family were in power. It was in this period that Verona's splendid townscape, which survives to this day, was mostly built. Although Verona did not lack poets and writers, the

city's greatest artistic achievements were in the field of sculpture and, particularly, architecture.

There are some outstanding examples of the Romanesque style in Verona such as the churches of the Holy Trinity (Santissima Trinità), St. Stephen (Santo Stefano), St. Laurence (San Lorenzo), St. Zeno, St. John in the Valley (San Giovanni in Valle), the Lower Church of San Fermo, etc. The Gothic style is exemplified by, among the churches, Sant'Anastasia, the greater part of the Duomo, San Fermo, and among non-religious buildings by the Castelvecchio, and the Arche Scaligere, or tombs of the Scala family. There is a great deal of very impressive sculpture in Verona, by unknown or little known craftsmen and stonemasons of the XIIIth and XIVth centuries. These men were primarily inspired by the great masters *Nicolò* and *Guglielmo*, but they were also open to other influences ranging from Venetian and Byzantine to the Wiligelmic, Carolingian and Ottonian. The finest products of this group of sculptors are the magnificent doors of the Duomo and San Zeno, and the XIVth Cent. monument to the Scala family, towering over which stands the impressive statue of Cangrande della Scala on horseback.

The earliest frescoes of note are the ones in the Chapel of St. Nazaire, (San Nazaro), painted in the Xth Cent. and even these early attempts are outstanding. Later frescoes, such as the early XIVth Cent. ones, clearly show the

Panorama of the Roman Theatre.

influence of Giotto and examples of these are to be found in San Fermo. There was, however, no distinct "School of Verona" as such, until the middle of the XIVth Cent. when Turone effectively founded the Veronese "school". He was followed by Altichiero, the famous artist, who worked both in Padua and Verona. As a result of Verona's unique position as an intermediary amongst widely diverse cultures, the city became one of the main centres of the International Gothic movement during the late XIVth and XVth Cents., Stefano da Verona and Pisanello were among the most outstanding painters of this period, Pisanello being a particularly brilliant medallionist. The Renaissance movement reached Verona rather late, in the mid- XVth Cent., and with it came *Andrea Mantegna*, who had begun his painting career ten years earlier in Tuscany. From then on, all the painters working in Verona remained to a greater or lesser extent under the influence of Mantegna, until examples of Bellini's and later Giorgione's and Titian's styles started coming in from Venice. In the XIVth and XVth Cents., Verona produced many famous artists, such as *Domenico* and *Francesco Morone, Liberale da Verona, Francesco Benaglio, Girolamo dai Libri*, the two *Caroto brothers, Francesco Bonsignori, Cavazzola, Niccolò Giolfino, Michele da Verona*, to name but a few. Later artists include *Francesco Torbido, Bonifacio de' Pitati*,

the two *Brusasorcis*, and *Antonio Badile*. During the late XVIth Cent., the influence of Mannerism became visible in the work of Paolo Farinati, and in the work of others of the School of Verona. This was the period in which Verona gave Venice one of her most famous sons: one of the greatest painters of the century – Paolo Caliari, called "Veronese". Fra' Giovanni, a monk belonging to the Order of the Mount of Olives, was responsible for the breathtaking wooden inlay work in the interiors of the churches of Santa Maria in Organo, and Monteoliveto Maggiore, near Siena.

The sculptor Antonio Rizzo did most of his best work in Venice, but the artist whose work is most remarkable in XVIth Cent. Verona is the military and civilian architect Michele Sanmicheli. He worked throughout the widespread Republic of Venice, spending a good deal of time in Verona. As well as being responsible for the walls which defended the city, Sanmicheli enriched the town with graceful palaces, imposing gateways, and his masterpiece, the Cappella Pellegrini. During the Renaissance period many of Verona's sons distinguished themselves in the arts and sciences. During the Baroque period, there wasa decline in the artistic activity of both Verona and Venice. Despite this, there are many famous names which make their appearance during this period, XVIIIth Cent. Verona saw the rise of various Academies, which

World War, and was among the most badly damaged of all Italian cities.

Despite the natural and man-made disasters which Verona has experienced throughout its history, it has emerged as one of the foremost cities in Italy, and looks forward to an increasingly prosperous future.

A brief glance at the culture and art of Verona during the XIXth and XXth Cents. shows that the town did not lag behind in modern developments and ideas. The XIXth Cent. saw the rise of poets such as Ippolito Pindemonte, Aleardo Aleardi and Antonio Cesari, who devoted himself to trying to improve the Italian language by attempting a revival of its Medieval purity. Other distinguished artists were architects such as Barbieri and Giuliari, sculptors like Della Torre and Fraccaroli, and painters such as Canella and Cabianca. The late XIXth and early XXth Cents. saw an upsurge of Traditionalism in Veronese art. The history of Verona has now reached modern times, and it is not necessary to mention a long list of important, living artists to prove that Verona still holds its own as an artistic and cultural centre.

Tufo relief carving of S. Martin (Castelvecchio Museum); below **the fifteenth century edicola of the Virgin near the "Wing" of the Arena.**

produced many very distinguished men.

The arrival of Napoleon and the French, and the fall of the Venetian Republic at the end of the XVIIth Cent. brought an abrupt change of the history of Verona. Many decisive battles were fought in the area around the city, including those of Arcole and Rivoli. Against the invading Jacobins, the Veronese people, true to the traditions of Venice and Catholicism, rose in a rebellion known as the "Pasque Veronesi" (Veronese Easter), so called because it took place over Easter in the April of 1797. Thereafter, the town was captured by the Austrians and in 1801 it was split between Austria and France. In 1805, it became a part of the Kingdom of Italy, but finally returned under Austrian domination in 1814. This marked the beginning of a long and irksome subjection to Austria. This period was, however, punctuated by bold attempts at rebellion and conspiracies, which resulted in the death of patriots such as *Carlo Montanari*, born in Verona and hanged at Belfiore in March 1853. This period was also punctuated by important battles which took place in the neighbourhood of the city: the battles of Santa Lucia and Custoza in 1848, San Martino and Solferino, then the Peace of Villafranca in 1859, and a second battle of Custoza in 1866. Throughout this time there was much sacrifice and boodshed, which only came to an end when the city finally became part of Italy again on the 16th October, 1866. Then began the long patient struggle to recover lost time and opportunities. Verona had to recoverfrom the heavy military demands made upon it in the years of virtual bondage, when the city was the principal fortress of the *Quadrilatero*, a defensive system based on a square formation, with Verona, Peschiera, Mantua and Legnano at each corner. The city then had to carve out a new future for itself. In 1882, it was devastated following the flooding of the River Adige. In the years 1915-1918 it was in the front line of the First

Porta Nuova by Michele Sanmicheli; below: *The Della Bra Gates.*

THE APPROACH TO THE TOWN

The most widely used and convenient approaches to Verona are from the south: exits from the "Serenissima" and Brenner autostradas and the junction of two main roads, the 11 and 12. The approach from this direction takes the visitor past the industrial area and the exhibition grounds, and the Porta Nuova railway station. The meeting place for the traffic converging on Verona from the south is the vast Porta Nuova square, just outside the circle of the walls built by the Venetians and the Austrians, which still surround the city. It is here that Verona really begins.

The massive *Porta Nuova*, through which the visitor enters this side of the city, is a monument to the genius of Michele Sanmicheli. The Porta Nuova was built between 1535 and 1540, but only part of what is now standing is original, as some of it was rebuilt by the Austrians in 1854.

"Listone della Bra"; below ***Palazzo Gran Guardia.***

PIAZZA BRA

Piazza Bra is the largest square in Verona, in fact one of the most spacious and impressive in the whole of Italy. One enters the Piazza through an archway known as the *Portoni della Bra*, consisting of two huge arches surmounted by battlements which formed part of the walls built by Gian Galeazzo Visconti at the end of the XIVth Cent. This gateway is flanked on one side by the *Torre Pentagona*, which was also built at the end of the XIVth Cent. The centre of Piazza Bra is occupied by public gardens, containing a statue erected in 1883 to *Vittorio Emanuele II*, as well as a more recent one erected in honour of the *Partisans* of the Second World War. Many of the buildings which form three sides of the square are of great architectural importance. The *Palazzo della Gran Guardia*, the first building on the left of the "Portoni", although similar in style to the work of Sanmicheli was, in fact, built in 1610 by Domenico Curtoni. The Palace remained incomplete until 1820, and is notable for its massive bulk, as well as the forceful design of the façade, the doorway, and the windows. After the Palazzo della Gran Guardia comes the Neoclassical *Palazzo Barbieri*, otherwise known as the "Nuova Gran Guardia" which now houses the municipal offices. It was built in 1838 by G. Barbieri in the then fashionable classical style. On the left is the *Amphitheatre*. The fourth side of the square has a gracefully curving line of buildings. The line of the buildings is further emphasised by a very wide pavement, known as the *Listone*, and it is here that the people of Verona like to take an evening stroll. Among these buildings, the most important architecturally is the *Palazzo Guastaverza*, designed by Sanmicheli.

Palazzo Barbieri; below *the fountain in Piazza Bra.*

The entrance to the Museo Lapidario Maffeiano; gravesite stele of a married couple, Roman period.

MUSEO LAPIDARIO MAFFEIANO

This is reached through a passage under the arcade of the Filarmonico, near the Portoni della Bra. Founded by the Veronese scholar Scipione Maffei in 1714, it is the oldest museum in Europe devoted to a collection of ancient inscriptions. In the open gallery, designed by the architect A. Pompei, there is an outstanding exhibition of stone slabs bearing inscriptions, statues, funeral urns, and bas-reliefs, most of them Etruscan, Greek or Roman, with a few Medieval fragments. The collection was catalogued and described by Maffei himself in his publication *Museum Veronense*, 1749.

Entrance courtyard, Museo Lapidario Maffeiano; below *statue of a woman and funerary stele.*

The Roman Amphitheatre, better konwn as the "Arena"; opposite page: *the "Wing" or "Ala".* Following pages: *aerial view of the Arena.*

THE ARENA

The Roman Amphitheatre, better known as the "Arena", is the most important of the monuments for which Verona is famed, and of which the city is so justly proud. Originally, the Amphitheatre stood outside the Roman walls of the city. In the IIIrd Cent.B.C. however, the Emperor Gallienus extended the latter, to include The Arena, which is thought to have been built at the beginning of the Ist Cent. In size and importance it is second only to the Colosseum in Rome. It covers an elliptical site measuring 456 feet by 360 feet, and the dimensions of the pit are 243 feet by 144 feet. The main bulk of the structure is built of massive stones mortared together. The central core is faced with brick and stone quarried from the hills around Verona, and this combination of materials produces an attractive colour contrast. Very nearly the whole of the perimeter wall of the building has disappeared, so that today all that remains is two tiers of arches built of rose coloured stone. Although it was never meant to be seen like this, the overall effect is extremely pleasing. In fact, most of the architecture in Verona built during the Renaissance was inspired by the Arena, the city's crowning glory. The

Two views inside the Arena.

perimeter wall fell into ruin or was deliberately destroyed over the centuries, and all that remains today is the fragment that towers above the arena, composed of three tiers with only four arches remaining on each tier. This is known to the people of Verona as the *Ala*, or wing. The interior of the Arena is very impressive. From the pit, one looks up at flight upon flight of giant size terraces, which sweep upwards in ever widening circles. The pride which the people of Verona take in this, the most famous of their monuments is shown by the care lavished on the building. This pride first became evident in the late XVIth Cent. when a special council was set up, known as the *Conservatores Arenae*. This council was responsible for completely rebuilding the triple ring of internal arches supporting the terraces, and for the care of the 73 supports which radiate outwards and form the backbone of the structure.

The Amphitheatre of Verona served as a theatre for gladiatorial games, races, and other spectacular events. Since 1913 the Arena is the regular setting for splendid operatic performances.

This page: *two operas performed at the Arena*.

Piazza Erbe.

PIAZZA ERBE

Piazza Erbe is more or less where the *Forum* of the Roman town was. The Piazza is one of the most picturesque in Italy. It epitomises the character and atmosphere of Verona, with its lively and colourful fruit and vegetable market, covered by its world-famous giant umbrellas, the delightful variety of styles of the buildings surrounding it and its historically famous and centrally placed statues.

Starting from the south-western side of the square (from the corner of Via Mazzini), after the tall houses of the old Ghetto, one comes to a low building with its battlements and porticos. It was formerly the *Domus Mercatorum*, a magnificent Romanesque building, designed in 1301 by Alberto I della Scala, and extensively altered in the XIXth

Cent. At the far end of the square stands the impressive *Palazzo Maffei*, built in 1668, a dignified structure surmounted by a balustrade supporting six statues of mythical gods and goddesses (Hercules, Jupiter, Venus, Mercury, Apollo and Minerva). Apart from its beautiful statues, there is a lovely spiral staircase in the courtyard. To the left of Palazzo Maffei, is the square, lofty bulk of the *Torre del Gardello*. Cansignorio della Scala had it built in brick in 1370 and the bell-shaped, battlemented belfry was completed in 1626.

On the north-east side, the first building is the picturesque *Casa Mazzanti*, decorated with frescoes of mythological subjects by A. Cavalli in the XVIth Cent. (recently restored). Next to the Casa Mazzanti is the *Domus Nova*, whose original design has been considerably altered over the years. After the "Arco della Costa" (Arch of the Rib), so called because of the whale rib which hangs beneath it, is the *Palazzo del Comune*. The Medieval façade on this side of the Palazzo was concealed in the XIXth Cent. by G. Barbieri, under a Neo-classical one. The Palazzo is flanked by the *Torre dei Lamberti*, which rises 274 feet above the square, and is the tallest in Verona. It was begun in 1172 and completed in 1464, with the construction of the octagonal belfry, which still houses two ancient bells, the *Rengo* and the *Marangona*.

On the central island of the marble paved square, among the market stalls are several interesting statues. The first of them is a Lion of St. Mark on its XVIth Cent. *column*. The original statue was destroyed by the Jacobins in the XVIIIth Cent. but was replaced by a copy at the end of the XIXth Cent. Then we come to the *Fountain of Madonna Verona*, which Cansignorio commissioned in 1368: a column decorated with heads and symbolic figures in relief and supporting a Roman statue rises out of a circular basin from which the water overflows into a wider and lower one. Next we come to a small, square, shrine-shaped structure once used during the ceremonies of investiture, when citizens were elected to public office. This edifice is commonly known as the "Berlina".

The "Berlina" a sixteenth century edicola; below: *the Lion of St. Mark on the column in Piazza Erbe and a detail of the Roman statue on the Fountain of Madonna Verona.*

Preceding page: *the Fountain of Madonna Verona, built by Cansignorio in 1368*; above: *Juliet's famous balcony;* right: *bronze statue of Juliet by N. Costantini.*

JULIET'S HOUSE

(Via Cappello). – Verona is world famous as the setting for Shakespeare's Romeo and Juliet. Here the love story is brought vividly to life because quite a number of buildings mentioned in the play can still be seen in Verona today. *Juliet's house*, for instance, is in Via Cappello, not far from Piazza Erbe. It is a tall building, which probably dates back to the XIIIth Cent., with a mellow brick façade. Tradition in Verona has it that this was the house of the Capulets, the powerful Veronese family to which Juliet belonged. From the internal courtyard, which was recently restored and around which the house is built, one can see the famous balcony which plays such an important part in the legend.

Piazza dei Signori with the monument to Dante Alighieri; below: *Porta Bombardiera.*

PIAZZA DEI SIGNORI

Despite its proximity to Piazza Erbe, and the fact that it almost forms part of the same complex, Piazza dei Signori is totally different in shape, style and atmosphere. This Piazza was once described, somewhat romantically, as the "drawing room" of Verona, and it is true that it is probably the most distinguished and elegant place in the whole city, perhaps because of its peace and the harmony of the surrounding buildings.

Entering from Piazza Erbe, the *Palazzo del Comune* is on the right. The Romanesque façade of this tall building received considerable additions during the Renaissance period. It has the distinctive alternating bands of brick and stonework which can be considered the *leit-motiv* of the city as a whole. After a tall crenellated tower dating back to the second half of the XIVth Cent. is the *Palazzo del Capitano*, which has a XVIth Cent. façade, and a splendid entrance by Sanmicheli of the same century. In the courtyard stands the famous *Porta Bombardiera* built in 1687. The Piazza is bounded by the *Palazzo degli Scaligeri*, now the Prefecture. The original building dates from the XIIth Cent., but through the years it has been extensively altered. The façade itself, with its battlements in the style prevalent during the Ghibelline period, is the result of fairly recent restoration work. The *courtyard* is of particular interest, with its lovely Renaissance well, and *Gothic open gallery*, which was once decorated with frescoes done by Altichiero in the XIV Cent. Both this Palazzo and the nearby Church of Santa Maria Antica have close associations with Dante who found his "first refuge and welcome" in the home of the Scala family.

The most important monument in the Piazza dei Signori is, however, the splendid *Loggia del Consiglio*, built between 1476 and 1493. The attribution of the building to the Veronese architect Fra' Giocondo is somewhat uncertain. This is the most outstanding of all the Renaissance buildings in Verona, where an almost Tuscan simplicity of line blends with subtle decorative work and a warmth of colour reminiscent of Venetian architecture. The statues crowning the building, by Alberto da Milano, represent *Catullus*, *Pliny*, *Marcus*, *Vitruvius*, and *Cornelius Nepos*.

The XVIIIth Cent. façade of the *Domus Nova*, with its grand central arch is on the other side of the Piazza. This building houses the *Caffé Dante*, which is unique in that it still maintains the original XIXth Cent. interior decoration. A statue of *Dante*, by Ugo Zannoni (1865), Stands in the centre of the square.

The statue of Girolamo Fracastoro; below: **the Loggia del Consiglio, a Renaissance structure attributed to Fra' Giocondo.**

Tomb and equestrian statue of Cangrande I della Scala, masterpieces of fourteenth century Veronese sculpture; following page: **the Tomb of Cansignorio by Bonino da Campione and Gaspare Broaspini.**

SANTA MARIA ANTICA AND THE SCALA TOMBS

The church of the Scala family was very near to their city palace, and outside it they built their family cemetery.

Their church was Santa Maria Antica, a very old church founded in the VIIth Cent. and although it is small, the interior is very beautiful. It is a splendid example of Romanesque architecture in Verona, and has the distinctive Veronese facing consisting of alternating bands of brick and stone with cobblestone finishing inside. The church tower is surmounted by a very fine square belfry, which has Gothic mullioned windows and a conical tiled roof. Over the side-door there is the *tomb of Cangrande I della Scala*, who died in 1329. This also serves as a porch and is one of the best examples of XIVth Cent. sculpture in Verona.

Under a Gothic canopy, supported by columns and topped by a pyramid shaped roof is the tomb of Cangrande I, decorated with high relief sculpture. The statue of the dead prince lies on top of his tomb on a couch. The famous monument is unique, however, because of the statue of *Cangrande on horseback* which stands on top of its pyramid roof. The statue is the masterpiece of an anonymous XIVth Cent. sculptor known as the "Master of the Scala Tombs" (Maestro delle Arche Scaligere). This sculptor has portrayed the smiling horseman in vigorous and realistic style on his alert steed caparisoned for tournament. The original statue is now in the Castelvecchio Museum. The monument to Cangrande is the only one outside the marble enclosure, surrounded by its splendid wrought-iron fence, which carries the emblem of the Scala family. All the other tombs are within the enclosed area, many in the shape of a sarcophagus on the ground. One of these is the *tomb of Giovanni delle Scala* (who died in 1359) by Venetian stonemasons. Next to the entrance gate stands the *monument to Mastino II*, built between 1340 and 1350. It is raised on columns, and like the earlier monument to Cangrande the tomb lies under a Gothic canopy with decorated finials, surrounded by four small tabernacles, its pyramid crowned by the statue of the prince on horseback. The tomb itself is carved in high relief with figures of angels at each corner.

We now come to the most ornate of all the Scala family tombs – that of *Cansignorio*, who died in 1375. It is by Bonino da Campione and Gaspare Broaspini, and although it is based on the same architectural plan as the others, the workmanship is superior. The ornate decorations on the canopy were sculpted with remarkable skill and delicacy, so that the end result is like an immense and intricately elaborate ivory carving. The side tabernacles are particularly remarkable – as well of course – as the work on the tomb itself. The Scala family monuments are the supreme Gothic art achievement in Verona.

Romeo's house; following page: *the apse of Sant'Anatasia.*

ROMEO'S HOUSE

(Via delle Arche Scaligere). – This fine Medieval building is popularly identified with the *House of the Montecchi*, or Montagues, Romeo's family. The house is built of brick, and there are still traces of the original battlements, although it is now in such bad condition that no visitors are allowed into the inner courtyard.

SANT'ANASTASIA

The largest church in Verona was founded by the Dominicans in 1290 and completed in 1481. It is built on the site of an older and much smaller church likewise dedicated to St. Anastasia, of which nothing remains save the name. The decoration on the lofty façade is unfinished and only covers the lower portion of the

The façade of Sant'Anastasia and the lovely double ogival door; below: *one of the unusual holy water founts in Sant'Anastasia, known as the "gobbi", or "hunchbacks".*

building on each side of the impressive portal. Access to the church is through the mullioned twin – ogival arched doorway. The doors are framed by gracefully fluted narrow pillars of variously coloured marble rising to form a Gothic arch above the mullioned aperture. The carving on the architrave dates from the XIVth Cent. and resembles the decorative work on the Scala family tombs. The frescoes above, however, date from the early XVth Cent. and are much deteriorated. The bas-reliefs on the right pillar, representing *Episodes from the Life of St. Peter the Martyr*, are XVth Cent. too. The church possesses a high, mellow brick *bell-tower* built in the XVth Cent.

THE INTERIOR. – One of the most outstanding examples of Gothic church architecture in Verona. All the craftsmen were local. Its proportions and various elements of its design, however, are still markedly Romanesque. The stylised paintings of plants which decorate the dome are worthy of note. The floor was designed by Pietro da Porlezza in 1462. In front of the first column facing the nave are *holy water stoups* supported by human figures in a crouched sitting position, known as the "hunchbacks" of St. Anastasia.

THE RIGHT AISLE. – The first altar, commissioned by the *Fregoso Family*, was designed by Danese Cattaneo in 1565. The second chapel dedicated to *St. Vincenzo Ferreri*, and attributed to Pietro da Porlezza, contains

The interior of Sant'Anastasia.

delicate marble relief work. On the upper part of the wall there is a XVth Cent. fresco while the altarpiece, portraying *St. Vincenzo Ferreri*, is by P. Rotari (XVIIIth Cent.) The third chapel is designed on the same plan as the preceding one, and the lunette contains a painting of the *Deposition from the Cross* by Liberale da Verona, dating from the XVth Cent. The fourth chapel is reminiscent of Verona's Roman Arch of the Gavi. The altarpiece shows *St. Martin* painted by Fr. Caroto, and the painting of *Mary Magdalen* above it is by Liberale. The sixth chapel is known as the *chapel of the Crucifixion*. The bas-relief decoration is by P. da Porlezza. It contains the *Funeral monument to Gianesello da Folgaria* (about 1425) and *Pietà*, with figures in painted stone. At the end of the right *transept* is the beautiful *altar* dedicated to St. Thomas Aquinas. The altarpiece is by Girolamo dei Libri, and shows a *Madonna and Child with Angels*.

THE TRANSEPT houses five altars, including the high altar. The first chapel on the right, known as the Cavalli Chapel (*Cappella Cavalli*), contains the only non-fragmentary fresco in Verona which can be definitely attributed to Altichiero; the mural is therefore of great interest and shows the *Cavalli Family before the Virgin*. It was painted around 1390. The frescoes on the pillars and the one in the lunette above the *Tomb of Federico Cavalli* date from the early XVth Cent. and are by Martino da Verona. *St. George saving the Princess from the Dragon*, Pisanello's most famous fresco, used to be above the arch of the second chapel in the transept, known as the

Cappella Pellegrini. (It is now in the sacristy to the left of the transept). The walls of the chapel are completely covered with *terracotta panels* depicting *Scenes from the Life of Christ*, the most important work of Michele da Firenze dating from 1435.

The elegant Gothic *Main Chapel* contains the XIVth Cent. fresco of *the Last Judgement* on the right hand wall, and the impressive *Tomb of Cortesia Serègo* built in 1424-1429. This tomb is surrounded by an outstanding fresco depicting *The Annunciation* in the "International Gothic" style, attributed to Michele Giambolo.

THE LEFT AISLE. – The *Rosary Chapel* (Cappella del Rosario) is built in lavish late XVIth Cent. style and contains paintings by Veronese artists of the Baroque era, together with contemporary sculpture. Above the XIVth Cent. table altar is the *Madonna of the Rosary*, protector of the town. Next comes the *Miniscalchi Chapel* (XVIth Cent.); the *lunette* fresco is by Francesco Morone and the panel painting of the *Pentecost* is by N. Giolfino (XVIth Cent.). The third altar on the left (at the entrance) is dedicated to *St. Raymond*, and the altarpiece is a *Madonna and Saints* by D. Brusasorci (XVIth Cent.). The second altar on the left is dedicated to *St. Erasmus*, and the altarpiece is *Christ and Saints* by Nicolò Giolfino. The *Tomb of Guglielmo di Castelbarco* stands in the Piazza di Sant'Anastasia on the left of the façade as one faces the church. It was built around 1320, and anticipates the delicate structure of the Arche Scaligere.

The façade of the Cathedral with the double-arched portico; following page: *the portal in the Veronese Romanesque style by Maesto Nicolò.*

THE CATHEDRAL (DUOMO)

Santa Maria Matricolare, the Cathedral of Verona, stands in a small square flanked by ancient buildings, which create a perfect setting for the lovely old church, that stands partly on the site of a very ancient and pre-existing basilica. It was consecrated in 1187, although building and decoration continued long after this date. The design of the façade is unusual because of its mixture of Romanesque and Gothic elements. There is a splendid *canopy* above the doorway, composed of two arches, one above the other. It is an example of the Romanesque style developed in Verona and the Po Valley, ascribed to Master Nicolò and his school, who built the entrance in 1138. The right hand side of the building, the only one

completely visible, is of great interest, with its lovely side door, as is also the *apse* with its excellent relief work executed by Veronese craftsmen. The belltower is still not complete, despite work carried out on it recently by the architect E. Fagiuoli. The XVIth Cent. middle section is by Sanmicheli.

THE INTERIOR. – Spacious and impressive. Two lines of powerfully ribbed pillars branch out to support the Gothic vaulting, dividing the nave from the aisles. The trompe-l'oeil architectural scenes in the first three chapels in both right and left aisles are by G. M. Falconetto and were painted in the XVIth Cent.

33

The inside of the cathedral; below: *The Assumption by Titian.*

RIGHT AISLE. – The second chapel contains the *Epiphany* by Liberale da Verona, and the *Descent from the Cross, with Four Saints* by N. Giolfino. The third chapel houses the XVIIIth Cent. *Transfiguration* by G. B. Cignaroli and the *death mask of Pope Lucius III*, (died 1185). At the end of the right aisle, in the Cappella Mazzanti, lies the *Tomb of Saint Agatha*, a masterpiece by a follower of Bonino da Campione, dated 1353. The church's *main chapel* contains remarkable frescoes painted in the dome of the apse and on the arches. The subjects are the *Annunciation*, and the *Acts of Mary and the Prophets*, painted by Fr. Torbido in the XVIth Cent from sketches by Giulio Romano. A marble choirscreen by Sanmicheli encloses the main chapel and presbytery.

LEFT AISLE. – The third chapel contains the *Madonna and Saints* by A. Brenzoni (1533), and the *Epitaph of Archdeacon Pacifico*, a famous Veronese personage of the IXth Cent. The first (*Nichesola*) Chapel, with carved decorations by the famous Venetian architect Sansovino, contains the famous altarpiece by Titian (ca. 1535), The *Assumption* (the only painting he actually worked on in Verona). Opposite, to the left of the entrance, is the *Nichesola Monument*, an important work by Jacopo Sansovino.

SAN GIOVANNI IN FONTE

(Next to the Duomo). This little church, which was once the Baptistery of the Cathedral, was founded in the VIIIth and IXth Cents. The existing structure which includes a nave, two aisles and three apses, dates from the first years of the XIIth Cent. Only the capitals of the columns of the earlier structure are still extant.

THE INTERIOR. – The church contains paintings by Veronese painters of the XVIth Cent. as well as the remains of XIIIth, XIVth and XVth Cent. frescoes. The magnificent octagonal *Baptismal Font* (ca. 1200), one of the most outstanding examples of Medieval Veronese sculpture, stands in the centre. It is made of a single block of pink marble and around the exterior of each of the eight sides of the font are sculpted in medium high relief scenes from the New Testament, six which, from the *Annunciation to the Shepherds* to the *Baptism of Christ*, bear a close resemblance to the style of Maestro Brioloto in his sculptures on the facade of San Zeno.

The interior of San Giovanni in Fonte and a detail of the christening font, a significant example of Medieval Veronese sculpture.

SANT'EUFEMIA

This great church was begun in 1275, and it was eventually consecrated in 1331, but its original structure was greatly altered throughout the succeeding centuries. The fine portal is XVth Cent., and there are two tall double windows. On the façade is the marble sarcophagus and the *Tomb of the Lavagnoli Family* (ca. 1550). On the left, there is the *Verità Family Tomb*. Romanesque *bell-tower*.

THE INTERIOR. – There is a central nave with ceiling decorated with modern frescoes. Second altar on the right: Altarpiece by F. Torbido showing *Saints Barbara, Anthony Abbot and Roch.* (XVIth Cent.). The third altar on the right contains the *Madonna and Six Saints by D. Brusasorci*. The seventh altar on the right *Madonna and Saint Thomas of Villanova* by Cignaroli (XVIIIth Cent.). The *Chapel of the Spolverini dal Verme* contains the frescoed *Voyage of Tobias*, *St. Ursula* and *Saint Lucy*, all by F. Caroto. On the left wall *Madonna and the Saints* by Moretto da Brescia, and the *Crucifixion* by F. Brusasorci.

The exterior and interior of Sant'Eufemia.

Porta Borsari with its dual arches.

PORTA BORSARI

This archway stands at the end of Corso Porta Borsari, and was the *decuman* gate of the Roman city. All one can see of the gate today is the façade, which faces towards Corso Cavour, as the building itself has now collapsed. This remnant of Roman Verona is next in importance to the Amphitheatre, and dates from the second half of the Ist Cent. The gateway, which formed part of the first circle of city walls, consists of the two original arches with their lintels, tympana, and columns, surmounted by a double row of windows. The decoration on these windows inspired the architects of the Renaissance period, from Sanmicheli onwards. The gate bears an inscription dating from 245 A.D. in which Verona is given its Roman name: COLONIA VERONA AUGUSTA.

The façade of San Lorenzo and a detail of the interior.

SAN LORENZO

(Corso Cavour) – This is one of the most beautiful and important churches in Verona. It is built on the site of an Early Christian basilica, some fragments of which are visible from the courtyard. One enters the courtyard from Corso Cavour, passing under an archway bearing a statue of St. Laurence. It was built about 1117, and soon afterwards considerably enlarged.

The exterior is in typical Verona Romanesque style, with alternating bands of brick and stone. The *porch* on the right and the *bell-tower*, which was restored quite recently, were both originally built in the second half of the XVth Cent. The church has a unique feature: the two *cylindrical towers* housing the spiral staircases leading up to the women's galleries.

The Gavi Arch.

GAVI ARCH

This Roman arch stands in a small square at the end of Corso Cavour, to which it was transferred in 1930. Its original position was in the middle of the busy thoroughfare, near the clocktower of the Castelvecchio, from where it was removed and incorporated in the medieval city walls. It was broken up by the French in 1705.

The outside of Caselvecchio; following page: *the entrance.*

CASTELVECCHIO

The massive and crenellated Castelvecchio (Old Castle), formerly known as the Castello di San Martino, was built as a stronghold by Cangrande II della Scala in 1354-55. Incorporated in its structure was an extensive portion of the city walls, terminating at the River Adige. The castle has had a fairly eventful history as it has survived, though not unscathed, successive dominations by various ruling families, plus the Venetians, French and Austrians. The small fort in the inner courtyard was built by Napoleon. For obvious military reasons the castle was equipped with battlements and towers, which were removed as late as the 1930s, when the ancient building was given a new role as a museum. The irregular line of the external walls is punctuated by six roofed towers, one of which, taller and more strongly fortified than the others, is known as the *Mastio* (keep). The castle walls are bounded by a deep moat through which flowed the so-called "Adigetto" (or little Adige). The interior is divided by partition walls which separate it into three courtyards of varying sizes. Recent excavation has unearthed some interesting remains of the castle as it originally was, such as the *Morbio Postern Gate* part of the inner ramparts, and the remains of the tiny and ancient church of San Martino. The fort built by Napoleon underwent considerable changes between 1923 and 1926.

Inner courtyard of Castelvecchio; below: *another view of the courtyard and the entrance to the Museum of Castelvecchio.*

Two other views of the inner courtyard at Castelvecchio.

Interior of the Museum of Castelvecchio; below: *statue of St. Catherine, XIVth Cent.*

MUSEUM OF CASTELVECCHIO

The Castelvecchio has been almost fully restored to its original form, thanks to painstaking work begun in 1957, under the guidance of C. Scarpa and L. Magagnato. The reorganisation of the interior into a museum has been so well carried out that it is now considered one of the best laid out museums in the whole of Europe. The entrance to the museum is on the ground floor, with the offices and library.

ROOM 1. – Romanesque sculpture influenced by the Veronese style. *Sarcophagus of Saints Sergius and Bacchus*, 1179. XIIIth Cent. *male figure* attributed to Brioloto and a ciborium made in the shape of *Female figures supporting a stone slab*, dating from the XIIth Cent. The annex to this room contains an alcove of modern design, which houses a precious collection of Longobard jewellery, gold and bronze objects and late Medieval glass.

ROOM 2. – XIVth Cent. Veronese sculpture, including statues of *Saints Catherine, Cecilia, John the Baptist and Martha*, from the church of San Giacomo di Tomba.

ROOM 3. – XIVth Cent. Veronese sculpture, including *Madonna Enthroned with Child, Crucifixion, Madonna, St. Libera* and others.

The tomb of Saints Sergius and Bacchus, 1173; below: *St. Catherine, XIV Cent.*

ROOM 4. – Late XIVth Cent. Veronese sculpture – *Crucifixion* from San Giacomo di Tomba and the *Mary and Martha group* by the Master of Cellore.

ROOM 5. – Early XVth Cent. sculpture, including panels showing the *Prophets*, *St. Martin* (1436) and *St. Peter on a Bishop's Throne*.

ROOM 6. – (On the other side of the wall) Ancient *bells of Verona* dating from the XIVth to the XVIIIth Cents.

ROOM 7. – The Da Prato Collection of antique firearms.

ROOM 8. – XIIIth and XIVth Cent. *frescoes* from churches and palaces in Verona.

ROOM 9. – Salvaged XIVth Cent. frescoes – *Madonna and Child*, *the Coronation of the Virgin* and *Crucifixion*.

ROOM 10. – *The Holy Trinity, The Redeemer, The Crucifixion*, polyptychs by Turone, together with an anonymous XIVth Cent. altar front depicting *The Seven Saints*; Tommaso da Modena's *Saints and a Nun*, and the *Boi Polyptych* by the school of Altichiero.

ROOM 11. – Examples of the International Gothic School. This is one of the most important collections in the museum. The *Madonna of Humility, St. Jerome, the Resurrection*, all by Jacopo Bellini; the *Madonna of the Quail* by Pisanello, *the Madonna of the Milk* by M.

Madonna Enthroned and Crucifixion, XIV cent. Veronese sculpture; below *St. Libera, XIV Cent. and The Swooning Virgin, early XIV Cent.*

Crucifixion with the Virgin and Saint John the Evangelist from San Giacomo di Tomba, by the Master of Cellore; below: *Saint Mary, early XIV Cent., and the bell from the Gardello Tower cast by Master Giacomo.*

The Sala d'Armi, below: *Holy Trinity polyptych by Turone.*

Giambono, the *Madonna of the Rose Garden* and a *Madonna and Child* by Stefano da Verona.

ROOM 12. – Dedicated to the work of foreign artists.

ROOM 13. – XIVth and XVth Cent. paintings, including the *Death of the Virgin* by Giambono, a *Crucifixion* by Jacopo Bellini; the *Aquila Polyptych*, the *Ancona* (Altarpiece) *of the Francanzani*, the *Altarpiece of the Resurrection* and many other paintings by Giovanni Badile.

ROOM 14. – Paintings by Veronese artists of the Renaissance, including Liberale, Nicolò Giolfino, F. Verla, G. Moceto, Domenico Morone, and Giovanni Maria Falconetto.

ROOM 15. – Venetian masters of the Renaissance period. Outstanding among them is Giovanni Bellini, represented by two paintings of the *Madonna and Child*. Gentile Bellini's *Crucifix of Albarelli*, Vittorio Carpaccio's *Two Saints with a Page*, and works by Marco Basaiti, Giovanni Mansueti, and Bartolomeo Montagna.

ROOM 16. – Important works by Veronese Renaissance painters, namely Domenico and Francesco Morone and Francesco dai Libri.

ROOM 17. – Paintings by Francesco Buonsignori. *Allegory of Music, the Dal Bovo Madonna and Madonna in Adoration.* This room also houses works by Antonio Vivarini and Giovanni Francesco Caroto.

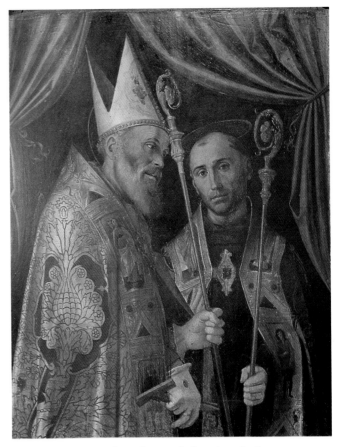

Saint Biagio and holy bishop by Bartolomeo Montagna; below: *the Sambonifacio chest with the Triumph of Chastity and the Triumph of Love by Liberale da Verona.*

Madonna of the Quail by Pisanello; next page: *Madonna of the Rose Garden, by Stefano da Verona.*

ROOM 18. – Dedicated primarily to Liberale da Verona, this room houses his *Adoration of the Shepherds*, the *Sambonifacio Dower Chest*, the *Madonna of the Goldfinch*, and a *Nativity*, as well as other works.

ROOM 19. Paintings by Andrea Mantegna. *Christ carrying the Cross, The Holy Family, Madonna and Child with St. Juliana*, This room also contains the *Madonna* by Carlo Crivelli, a *Holy Conversation* by Francesco Francia.

ROOM 20. – Ancient arms and fabrics belonging to Cangrande I, taken from his tomb at Santa Maria Antica. A covered passageway leads back into the main museum building, passing the concrete plinth on which the impressive original of the *Statue of Cangrande I on his horse* now stands.

ROOM 21. – Large *Polyptych* and *Four Saints* by Francesco Cavazzola. The room also holds *Madonna and Saints* by Giovanni Fr. Caroto, *Madonna Caliari* by N. Giolfino, and two exquisite panels, *A Young Monk* and *Child with a Drawing*, by Giovanni Francesco Caroto.

ROOM 22. – Devoted to works by Giovanni Francesco Caroto and Girolamo dai Libri. The most important example of the latter's work is the *Madonna Maffei*.

ROOM 23. – Works by the great Venetian artists of the XVIth Cent. *The Deposition from the Cross*, the *Bevilacqua Altarpiece, and Portrait of Pase Guarienti*, by Paolo Veronese. *Nativity, Madonna of the Milk*, and the *Concert*

Madonna of the Goldfinch by Liberale da Verona; below: ***fragment of the Madonna and Child by Francesco Bonsignori.*** Opposite page: ***Holy Family with a Saint by Andrea Mantegna.***

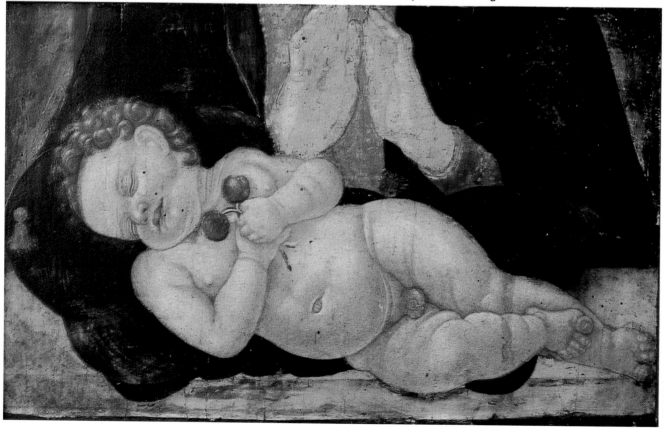

Deposition by Veronese; below Four Saints, late XVth cent; preceding page: *the original equestrian statue of Canagrande I, from the Scaligero Tombs.*

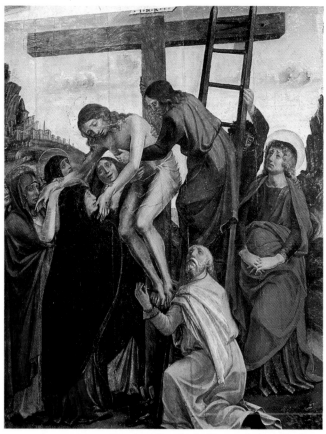

of the *Muses* by Jacopo Tintoretto. *St. Dorothy* by Sebastiano del Piombo, and paintings by Lorenzo Lotto and Bonifacio de' Pitati.

ROOM 24. – XVIth and XVIIth Cent. Veneto artists, especially Jacopo and Francesco Bassano, Paolo Farinati, Felice Brusasorci, Fr. Maffei, and Pasquale Ottino.

ROOM 25. – Paintings by Veronese and Venetian artists of the XVIIth Cent.

ROOM 26. – Veneto art of the XVIIth and XVIIIth Cents. Works by B. Strozzi, Ant. Balestra, G. Carpioni, Giambettino Cignaroli, and Dom. Feti. This room contains two works by G.B. Tiepolo, *Three Carmelite Monks and St. Theresa*, and his *Sketch* for the Ceiling of the Ca' Rezzonico, and also two *Capricci* by Francesco Guardi.

Note. – *The rooms of the Castelvecchio Museum are named after distinguished families or individual citizens of Verona, but these names have not been included in this guide.*

Deposition by Liberale da Verona; below: *Madonna and Child with St. Juliana by Andrea Mantegna, and Madonna of the Milk, by Jacopo Tintoretto.*

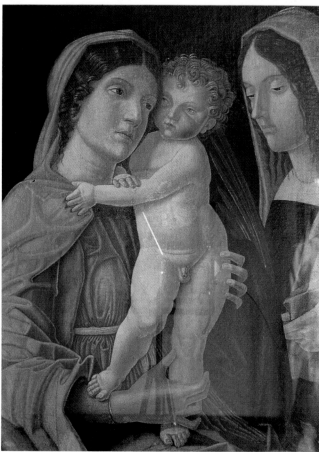

Capriccio, with a large country house on the shore of the Lagoon, by Francesco Guardi; below: *sketch for the ceiling of the Ca' Rezzonico by Tiepolo.*

Ponte Scaligero.

PONTE SCALIGERO

This famous bridge (named after the Scala family) forms part of the complex defence system of the Castelvecchio. Although its original purpose was purely military, it is nevertheless a masterpiece of Medieval design and engineering.

Built in 1355 by Cangrande II della Scala, its architect has been identified as Guglielmo Bevilacqua. The bridge has three great arches supported by solid turreted pilons – the widest boasting a 160ft. span. Both the arches and the towers as well as the tall battlements with forked merlons are chiefly built in brick.

The bridge presents a very imposing sight, with its glowing red brick, and the interior is no less impressive, giving fine views over the river and the city. Over the centuries, it was altered in many ways, and during the Second World War it was almost totally destroyed. However, reconstruction began immediately, and the bridge is now restored to its original splendour.

On the Ponte Scaligero; below: a picturesque view of the Adige River.

Rose window on the façade of San Zeno, by Master Brioloto; following page: *Piazza San Zeno with the basilica, belltower and XIIIth century rose window.*

SAN ZENO MAGGIORE

The Basilica of San Zeno Maggiore ranks with the Amphitheatre as one of Verona's most imporant monuments.

It is rightly considered one of the great achievements of Romanesque architecture. The present building is the third Basilica built on the same site. (The first church was built in the IVth/Vth Cents., the second in the Xth Cent.). The present church was commenced around 1120; shortly afterwards, the builders started enlarging it and work continued until the end of the XIVth Cent. The roof and the apse were rebuilt in the Gothic period.

The splendid *Façade* is perhaps the most outstanding of this period. It dominates an enormous paved square, and is flanked by a beautiful Romanesque *belltower* from the first half of the XIIth Cent., of superbly masterful design. On the other side stands the red XIIth Cent. *tower* of the ancient monastery mentioned by Dante in Canto 18 of his "Purgatory". The weathered Veronese stone of the church has a warm golden tone, and the restrained lines of the pillars, the columns, the cornices and the gallery with its double windows give the whole façade an air of harmonious elegance. The front of the building is crowned by a tympanum decorated with marble columns, and at each side, in typical Romanesque style, the roof continues on a lower level. The lovely large circular spoked rose *window*, surrounded by allegories of "Fortune", in the centre of the façade is by Master Brioloto. The tendency nowadays is to attribute to him not only the design of the window itself, but the design of the whole complex façade. On the cornices of the sloping side roofs, a carved frieze by Adamino da San Giorgio (early XIIIth Cent.).

The impressive *Portal* of the church dates from about 1138, and is generally attributed to Maestro Nicolò. It was incorporated in the present façade after the demolition of the earlier façade, to which it belonged. Above the

Bas-relief of St. Zeno among Infantrymen and Knights of the City Council, in the lunette above the door;
below: *detail of a caryatide on the porch.*

doors stands a *Portico* supported by columns on standing lions, and the lintels are decorated with carvings in relief, showing representations of the *Months of the Year*, by an unknown artist. On each side of the arch: figures of *St. John the Baptist* and *St. John the Evangelist*. *St. Zeno, among Infantrymen and Knights of the City Council* is sculpted in bas-relief in the lunette above the door. The eighteen bas-relief tablets on each side of the doorway also formed part of the earlier façade. They represent *scenes from the Old and the New Testaments*, the *Duel between Theodoric and Odoacer*, and bottom right, *Theodoric Hunting Evil Spirits*. The latter is thought to be the work of Nicolò, while the others are attributed to his pupil Guglielmo. The doors are unique in that each one bears 24 *Bronze Panels* depicting scenes from the *Old and New Testaments and the Miracles of Saint Zeno*. These panels are enclosed in borders of varied design with heads at each corner. In addition, the border of the right-hand door has the figures of six *Saints* and a *Sculptor*, while on the border of the left-hand door are 17 small panels depicting *Kings, Emperors*, and the *Virtues*. The bronze panels were transferred from the old doors when the entrance was enlarged during the early XIIIth Cent., and as a result, a few more had to be added

Above and below: details of the bas-reliefs on either side of the door.

Descent into Hell.
Beheading of Saint John.

Christ in Glory.
The Two Mothers.

The Expulsion form Eden.

Panel from the right-hand door; below: *St. Zeno and the messengers.*

First labors and fratricide.

On the this and the preceding page: **panels from the doors of San Zeno, XII-XIIIth cents.**

around this time. Most of them, however, were cast in the early XIIth Cent., and are attributed to a Veronese craftsman who came under the influence of Byzantine and markedly of Ottonian artists. Researchers are still trying to identifiy the author of the bronze panels, but the extraordinarily vivid, "barbaric" energy of the figures, the originality and freedom of the imagery employed is a superb blend of tradition and seething renewal.

The interior of San Zeno.

THE INTERIOR. – The interior of the church is a lovely combination of Romanesque and Gothic styles. The rigorous majesty of the structural elements stress the historical importance of this basilica. The spacious interior is divided by cruciform pillars and columns supporting sweeping arches. The central arch underlines the superb, tri-sectioned keel-shaped wooden ribbed *Gothic ceiling*. The church is built on three different levels: the *Lower Church*, occupying about two-thirds of the building, the *Upper Church* or raised Sanctuary, and the *Crypt* beneath. The few steps leading down into the church are flanked by two *holy water stoups*. To the left: a *Baptisimal Font* of monolithic design, attributed to Brioloto (XIIth Cent.).

RIGHT AISLE. – The walls and are covered with XIIIth and XIVth Cent. *frescoes*, of great importance in the history of

Veronese art of this period. They represent, among others, the following – *St. Christopher* (about 1300) and the *Madonna Enthroned*, by the "Second Master of San Zeno"; *Crucifixion and St. Stephen*, by the "First Master of San Zeno". Along the staircase and the wall of the raised Sanctuary are the *Madonna* by Martino da Verona, *St. George* by the "Second Master of San Zeno", and the *Baptism and Resurrection of Lazarus*, (XIIIth Cent.) and others. First altar on the right: *Madonna and Saints* by Fr. Torbido (XVIth Cent.). Second altar on the right: built of marble taken from a XIIIth Cent. portico.

THE SANCTUARY. – Statues of *Christ* and the *Apostles* by a local sculptor, who was influenced by the Saxon school,

Saint George by the "Second Master of San Zeno", and Madonna with Saints by Fr. Torbido, XIV Cent;
below: *Madonna Enthroned by the "Second Master of San Zeno".*

Detail of the Madonna from the triptych by Andrea Mantegna; following page: *statue of St. Zeno by an unknown XIV cent. artist.*

stand along the top of the iconostasis or balustrade. At the top of the right wall is a votive fresco dating from 1397. (School of Altichiero. The *Main Chapel*, constructed by Giovanni and Nicolò da Ferrara in 1386-1398, is decorated with frescoes by Martino da Verona. On the high altar stands the *Triptych*, the *Madonna and Saints* by Andrea Mantegna, painted between 1457 and 1459. In the left apse stands an impressive statue of *Saint Zeno*. It is made of multicoloured marble by an unknown sculptor of the early XIVth Cent., and is much loved by the people of Verona. Next to the Sacristy door stands

the *Statue of St. Proculus* by Giovanni da Verona (1392). On the wall is a *Crucifixion* which shows the influence of Altichiero, and two other versions of *the Crucifixion* by Turone and by the "Second Master of San Zeno". This wall also bears traces of many other frescoes.

THE CRYPT. – A broad staircase leads down to the crypt. The arches are decorated by friezes in relief, by Adamino da San Giorgio in 1225 (probably the year when the crypt was completed). The arches and vaults of the crypt are supported by 49 pillars, whose capitals are of great interest as each one is different. The central apse con-

Open shrine in the cloister of San Zeno; next page: *the apse and belltower of San Zeno.*

tains the urn holding the holy body of Saint Zeno. The crypt also contains several other sarcophagi, the most important being the XIIth and XIIIth Cent. ones of *St. Lupicillius, St. Lucillius* and *St. Crescentian.*

LEFT AISLE. – Baroque altar dedicated to Our Lady of Sorrows. At the end of the aisle, next to the entrance, stands the great monolythic porphyry bowl, probably of Roman origin. Legend, however, has it that the bowl was brought here by the devil. On the wall is the great *Crucifix* attributed to the Paduan artist, Guariento, and it is here that the "Carroccio" of the Veronese Commune was kept – when not in use – in the Middle Ages. The "Carroccio" was the war chariot on which the standard of the Free Commune of Verona was borne to the battlefield.

CLOISTERS. – One enters the cloisters from the left aisle of the basilica. The effect is one of spaciousness, as the covered walks surround a large open grassy square. The arches on two of the opposite sides of the cloisters are ogival, while those on the other two sides are rounded. A charming, open shrine with pillars and columns stands out from one of the sides of the cloister, which also houses stone fragments and tombs. On the eastern side the *Chapel of St. Benedict*, once probably a Roman hypogeum, or underground burial chamber, decorated with frescoes by the School of Giotto.

The cloister of San Bernardino; next page: **entrance to San Bernardino**.

SAN BERNARDINO

It used to belong to the Franciscan Order and was founded in 1451 and completed in 1466. It is preceded by a cloister. The façade is brick and has pointed Gothic windows. *Statues of Franciscan Saints* stand above the lunette that crowns the main entrance (1474), whereas the lunette itself contains a mural of the *Episode of St. Francis receiving the Stigmata.*

THE INTERIOR. – There is a single nave, a feature which is often found in Franciscan churches, as well as a side aisle and chapel on the right of the church. First chapel on the right: frescoes on the walls of *Episodes from the Life of St. John the Evangelist* by N. Giolfino, who also painted the *Episodes from the Life of St. Francis* on the ceiling vault. Over the altar hangs a copy of the original painting by Cavazzola, now in Castelvecchio. Second chapel on the right: *Madonna and Child with Saints*, by F. Bonsignori. Fourth chapel on the right: Frescoes by Dom. and Fr. Morone: The marble altarpiece depicts *Franciscan Saints.* Fifth chapel on the right: *The Crucifixion*, a masterpiece by Fr. Morone dating from 1498. Also, *Mary and Jesus* by Fr. Caroto, the *Resurrection of Lazarus* by A. Badile, and the *Story of the Passion*, by N. Giolfino. The *Deposition from the Cross* is a copy of the Cavazzola original now in Castelvecchio. Behind an iron railing stands a group in multicoloured stone, representing the *Lamentation over*

the Body of Christ. Cappella Pellegrini (Entrance to the right of the nave) built by Michele Sanmicheli around 1527 for Margherita Pellegrini. Sanmicheli used a centralized plan for his masterpiece. Lovely spatial proportions flow in classical stately harmony. Two orders, a cupola decorated inside in the Roman manner and supported by a drum (tiburium). The door and three altars open off the lower order. Niches and three-mullioned windows with columns succeed each other in the upper order. A *Madonna and Child with St. Anne* by B. India (1579) above the altar.

THE LEFT WALL. – The 1481 organ is beautifully decorated by Domenico Morone. The first altar is dedicated to the *Brasavola Family* and was designed by Fr. Bibiena in the XVIIIth Cent.. The altarpiece depicting *St. Peter of Alcantara* is by A. Balestra. A graceful XVth Cent. cloister is reached by a door in the left wall of the church. The lunettes in the cloisters are decorated with XVth and XVIth Cent. frescoes. The main cloisters lead to the ancient *Library* of the Monastery, completely covered with frescoes by Domenico and Francesco Morone dated 1503. The painting on the end wall depicts the *Madonna Enthroned* surrounded by members of the Sagramoso Family, on the side walls: the *Saints and Famous Members of the Franciscan Order.*

Church of the Santissima Trinità.

CHURCH OF THE SANTISSIMA TRINITA

An example of the Veronese Romanesque style, the church was founded in 1073, and was finally consecrated in 1117. Only the northern apse remains of the earlier building: the porch, the other apses, and the belltower were built around 1130. The square *Belltower*, with its brick and thinly banded stone facing and the elegant, three-mullioned windows of the bell-chamber is supposed to have inspired the builders of St. Zeno.

Tomb of Antonia da Sesso, 1421 and the interior of the Santissima Trinità church; below: ***Porta Palio.***

PORTA PALIO

This gateway takes its name from a *"Palio"* or horse-race which used to be run in the vicinity, mentioned by Dante in Canto 15 of the "Inferno". It was once known as the Porta di San Sisto and is Sanmicheli's masterpiece in his capacity as a military architect. The outer façade is built of smooth square-hewn stones rigorously partitioned by paired columns, while the inner consists of five arches, in which classical simplicity merge with delightful Mannerist decoration. Behind the arches is a gallery. The gateway was built between 1542 and 1557.

Cloister of San Francesco al Corso; left: *entrance to the former Monastery of the Capucins.*

JULIET'S TOMB

(Via del Pontiere). – The final goal of the pilgrim in search of Shakespeare's Romeo and Juliet is Juliet's tomb in the picturesque former monastery of the Capucins. Only the *cloisters* and the Baroque *Chapel of St. Francis* remain. The empty sarcophagus lies in a dimly lit crypt, and only reached this resting place after many vicissitudes. A long, but disputed tradition has it that this is the tomb of Shakespeare's heroine.

Juliet's tomb; below: *room with a statue of Torquato della Torre and frescoes by Brusasorzi and B. India.*

Top, from the left: *Washing of the Feet, by Francesco Caroto and Annunciation by Louis-Dorigny;* below: *Sala Guarienti by Paolo Farinati.*

Above: *Annunciation by Sigismondo De Stefani*; below: *Annunciation by Louis-Dorigny*; left: *Saint Catherine by Caroto.*

San Fermo Maggiore seen from the Ponte delle Navi; next page: *the apse.*

SAN FERMO MAGGIORE

In ancient times a small chapel stood on the banks of the river Adige, near the spot where St. Fermo and St. Rustico were martyred. It was rebuilt in the VIIIth Cent. and in the XIth Cent., the Benedictine Friars founded a much larger structure in which, from the start, one of the two churches erected on the site, was intended to be built above the other. The lower church, the two lesser apses and the belltower which was not completed until the XIIIth Cent. all belong to the Benedictine project. The date 1065, which appears in the lower church, probably refers to the year in which the Benedictine part was started;

whereas the building was restructured and given its present appearance by the Franciscans, who took over the complex after 1313. The great Gothic upper nave and the splendid apsidal complex were built above the pre-existing Romanesque lower church. The two styles merge into each other harmoniously, thanks to the unity of the colour-scheme maintained throughout the complex.

The absidal sector of the upper church has delightful interwoven decorations and richly ornamented arches.

THE FAÇADE. – The varied openings in the façade

The funeral monument to Aventino Fracastoro on the façade of San Fermo Maggiore; preceding page: *exterior of the church.*

progress, diminishing in scale, up to the point of the roof, from the great recessed *Main Door*, flanked by two *Porched Tombs* (Left: *Monument to Aventino Fracastoro* – doctor to the Scala family – who died in 1368; the frescoes which used to decorate the tomb are now in the museum of Castelvecchio – page 69. Right: the porched *Tomb of Giovanni da Tolentino*) and by mullioned ogival windows, to a great four-mullioned central window topped by a smaller three-mullioned window and two round port windows, above which a series of pensile arches define the simple hut-shaped top of the façade.
The usual entrance to the church is on the left where a staircase, covered by a massive porch, leads up to the door. XIIIth Cent. frescoes in the lunette (the one on the left by Fr. Morone, 1523).

INTERIOR OF THE UPPER CHURCH. – Of typical Franciscan design, with a single nave, it has a magnificent XIVth Cent. multi-keel-shaped wooden ribbed *ceiling*, decorated with images of saints. The church is primarily famous for the quality and number of its XIVth and XVth Cent. frescoes. In the lunette above the main door is the *Crucifixion*, attributed to Turone. On the opposite wall are fragmentary XIVth and XVth Cent. frescoes, including the *Last Judgement* by Martino da Verona.
THE RIGHT WALL. – XIVth Cent. fresco representing the *Martyrdom of Franciscan Friars*. Above the XVIth Cent. *Nichesola Altar* is a *Madonna and Saints* by S. Creara, while the lunette is by D. Brusasorci. The detached fresco – *Angels with a Scroll* is by Stefano da Verona. The *Pulpit* (1360) was commissioned by a lawyer, Barnaba da

The interior of San Fermo Maggiore.

Morano, and is surmounted by a Gothic canopy. The frescoes surrounding it are by Martino da Verona. The *Annunciation* – a fresco – on the upper section of the wall, clearly reveals Giotto's influence. On the walls of the Brenzoni Chapel (XVth Cent.) are the *Tomb of Bernardo Brenzoni* (died 1494), and the *Funeral Monument of Barnaba da Morano*, decorated with statues and fine reliefs, probably by a Venetian artist. The third altar, known as the *Saraina* (XVIth Cent.), used to be in the Church of the Holy Trinity (Santissima Trinità). On the altar front is a XVth Cent. *Deposition.* The fine altarpiece shows *The Holy Trinity, Madonna and Saints* and is by Fr. Torbido. The lines of the fifth altar were inspired by the Roman Gavi Arch.

RIGHT APSE. – *Crucifixion* by D. Brusasorci. Then comes the *Main Chapel*, highlight of the Basilica, in front of which there is a semi-circular screen (1523). Above the triumphal arch, frescoes (about 1314), depict the kneeling figures of *Prior Daniele Gusmerio* and *Guglielmo di Castelbarco*, and clearly reveal the influence of Giotto. There are other important XIVth Cent. frescoes on the wall: the *Coronation of the Virgin, Adoration of the Magi* and the *Stories of the Franciscan Friars*. Behind the XVIIIth Cent. main chapel altar there are rare wooden choirstalls (XVth Cent.). The vault of the ceiling above the apse is decorated with XIVth Cent. frescoes, depicting the *Symbols of the Four Evangelists*. Above the altar in the nearby *Chapel of St. Anthony* hangs Liberale da Verona's outstanding *Saints Anthony, Nicholas and Augustine. Monument to the Della Torre Family*, in the rectangular chapel beside the left wall, a splendid example of the sculpture of A. Briosco, called "Il Riccio", with richly carved marble sections and superb bas-reliefs in bronze. The originals of the bronze reliefs – now in the Louvre, in Paris – are replaced by copies.

THE LEFT WALL. – The Baroque *Lady Chapel*; above the altar, a *Madonna with Saints*, by Fr. Caroto. A 1363 fresco of the *Crucifixion* above the side door. The 1535 *Chapel of the Helmsmen* (Cappella dei Nocchieri) contains *Saints Nicholas, Augustine and Anthony Abbot*, by Battista Dal Moro, the famous *Monument to Nicolò Brenzoni* by the Florentine artist Nanni di Bartolo, who

Monument to Nicolò Brenzoni by Nanni di Bartolo, and XIVth century pulpit with frescoes by Martino da Verona.

The lower church of San Fermo Maggiore.

sculpteda *Resurrection* all around the urn between 1424 and 1426. In these years the great Pisanello painted one of his most famous frescoes on the surrounding wall – the *Annunciation.* Above it, subtly harmonising with the architectural lines, are the figures of the *Almighty* and the *Archangels Raphael* and *Michael.* This fresco is a masterpiece of the artist's early period and is of great importance in the study of northern Italian Gothic art.

THE LOWER CHURCH. – Built in 1065 or thereabouts, this church is an outstanding and rare example of early Veronese Romanesque architecture. The great nave is separated from the aisles by pillars. The main nave has double arches supported by a row of smaller pillars. The varied shapes of the ancient capitals are worthy of note, together with the XIIIth and XIVth Cent. frescoes which adorn the walls and the pillars.

PORTA DEI LEONI

(The Lion Gate, in Via Leoni). – Yet another monument bequeathed by the Romans, dating from the middle of the Ist Century B.C. It was once part of the ancient city walls, and was drastically altered about a hundred years after its construction. It consisted of two arches topped by a tympanum and flanked by columns, above which rose a series of arched windows, and finally a large exedra. The rear of the existing section is concealed by a building immediately behind it, but the visible part corresponds more or less to the centre of the original gate. This gate, which is one of the most precious mementos of Roman Verona, was much admired by the artists of the Renaissance period for its perfect proportions and the beauty of its ornamentation. Recent thorough archaeological diggings, the results of which are clearly visible from the street, have revealed the base of the ancient Roman gateway, extensive sections of the original road surface and the polygonal base of one of the great corner towers, defending the gateway.

Porta dei Leoni; below: *recent excavations at the Porta dei Leoni.*

Façade of the Palazzo Pompei, by Sanmicheli, now the Museum of Natural History.

PALAZZO POMPEI (MUSEUM OF NATURAL HISTORY)

Palazzo Pompei (Lungadige Porta Vittoria) – formerly known as Palazzo Lavezola, was built by the architect Sanmicheli, between about 1530 and 1550, when his reputation was already firmly established. It is one of his great works, and shows a very strong classical influence, despite concessions to the style of the time and the purpose of the building. The impressive façade, divided into two storeys, and the well-proportioned internal courtyard are of particular interest.

This Palazzo has long housed the *Museum of Natural History*, which is famous throughout Italy and Europe. There are over 20 rooms, containing rare collections, and the following fields are represented – mineralogy, paleontology, biology, ornithology, icthyology, entomology, etc.

Inner courtyard of the Palazzo Pompei; below: *Eocene fossils.*

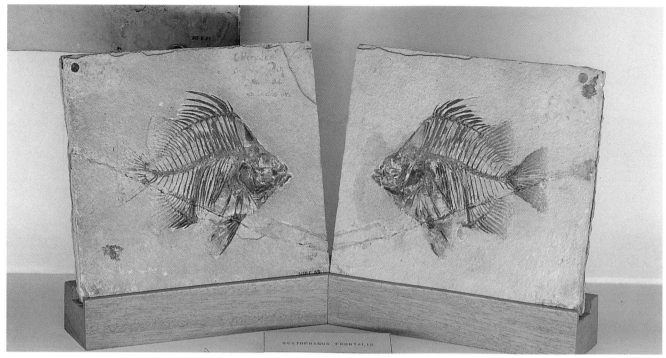

Scatophagus Frontalis.

Dombeyopsis.

Mammoth in the Quaternary Room.

These are some of the more important rooms: Room I contains a very fine collection of *Eocene fossils* from the Bolca region. This includes a large number of animal and plant species which existed more than 30 million years ago. Rooms II and III are dedicated to collections of *minerals* and *stones*. Rooms V, VI, VII, and VIII are devoted to *mammals*. Rooms IX, X, XI and XII are devoted to all aspects of *ornithology*. Rooms XIII and XIV contain exhibitions of *fish, reptiles* and *amphibians*. The collection of *insects* in Room XV is of great interest. The remaining rooms deal with *invertebrates, paleontology,* and *prehistory*, among other subjects.

Top, from the left: *petrified trunk and display case in the Mineral and Stone collection (Sala delle Rocce);* above, from the left: *Papagoite and showcase in the Mushroom Collection (Sala dei Funghi);* below: *Stratigraphic Geology exhibit.*

Façade of the Church of Santi Nazaro e Celso: preceding page: **entrance to the church courtyard.**

SANTI NAZARO E CELSO

(Largo San Nazaro). – This church, built between 1464 and 1483, was once part of a Benedictine monastery. A large cloistered courtyard in front of it, has an imposing entrance built in 1688.

THE INTERIOR. – A main nave flanked by two aisles with three apses.

RIGHT AISLE. – The *Annunciation*, by P. Farinati (1557) hangs above the second altar. *Adam and Eve* in the lunette are by the same painter. *Ecce Homo*, by O. Flacco, above the fourth altar.

SACRISTY. – The XVth Cent. wall *cupboards* are decorated with marquetry. There is a XVth Cent. triptych depicting the *Pietà and Saints Benedict and Francis*. The *Madonna and Saints* is by F. Brusasorci. The sections of a polyptich by Bartolomeo Montagna show *Saints Blaise and Juliana* and *Christ on the Sepulchre*. The Main Chapel contains impressive *frescoes* and four paintings depicting

Episodes from the Life of St. Celsus by P. Farinati. There are another two pieces by Montagna, representing *Saints Benedict and John the Baptist*, and *Saints Nazarus and Celsus*.

The Chapel of San Biagio, in the left transept, was built by the architect Beltramo di Valsolda in 1488, and consecrated in 1529. Above the main arch is a painting of the *Annunciation* by P. Cavazzola (1510). There is a splendid marble altar with the *Sarcophagus of Saints Blaise and Juliana* by Bernardino Panteo (1508), altarpiece by Fr. Bonsignorio (the *Martyrdom of Two Saints*, and a *predella* by Girolamo dai Libri).

LEFT AISLE. – The fifth chapel contains the *Madonna and Saints* by Dom. Brusasorci. In the third chapel there is the *Miracle of Saint Maurus* by G. Carpioni, and the *Madonna in Glory with Saints* by Antonio Badile is in the second chapel.

Views of the Giusti Gardens, a splendid example of Late Renaissance Italian gardens.

GIUSTI GARDENS

This garden belongs to the XVIth Cent. *Palazzo Giusti*. It is one of the finest late Renaissance gardens in the whole of Italy, and dates from 1580. It is divided into two sections – the lower part being in the Italian style. The layout is spacious, with flower beds, a maze, statues, fountains etc., and a cypress avenue winding up the small hill topped by the Church of San Zeno in Monte, which was much admired by Goethe. There is a tower-shaped building with a winding staircase and a platform on top, from which one enjoys a magnificent view over the city.

The façade of Santa Maria in Organo.

SANTA MARIA IN ORGANO

(Piazza Santa Maria in Organo). – This church belonged to the monks of the Order of the Mount of Olives, and was re-designed in its present form in 1481. The lower part of the façade was built over an older original, and is attributed to Sanmicheli. The *Belltower*, however, with its domed top, was designed by Fra Giovanni da Verona.

THE INTERIOR. – It is in Renaissance style, and has a nave, two aisles and a raised presbytery. The walls of the central nave are decorated with frescoes depicting *Stories from the Old Testament*, those on the right by Francesco Caroto, and those on the left by N. Giolfino.

RIGHT AISLE. – *Madonna and Saints* by Antonio Balestra in the first chapel and the *Journey of St. Joseph* by G.B. Pittoni (XVIII Cent.). *St. Michael* by P. Farinati in the second chapel.

PRESBYTERY. – In the chapel opening off the end wall, on the right, flanked by frescoes by Cavazzola, *Santa Francesca Romana*, an altarpiece by Guercino (1639). The chapel to the right of the main Chapel contains frescoes by N. Giolfino, and Cavazzola's *Annunciation*. In the left chapel are *frescoes* by D. Brusasorci and *St. Benedict* by S. Brentana. Above the altar at the end of the left wall is the *Blessed Bernardo Tolomei* by L. Giordano.

The *Main Chapel*. Paintings of the *Slaughter of the Innocents* and *Episodes from the Lives of Saints Gregory and Peter* by P. Farinati. Lower down, on one side, is a series of little *Landscapes* by Domenico Brusasorci.

The choir of Santa Maria in Organo; below: **marquetry in the choirstalls.**

CHOIR AND SACRISTY. – In this part of the church are the greatest works of Fra Giovanni da Verona – the superb multi-coloured wooden marquetry, the most outstanding of its type to be found in Italy. It was carried out in the late years of the XVth Cent. and in the early XVIth Cent. and consists of two rows of *choir stalls* in the lovely *Choir.* Fra Giovanni was the architect of the *Sacristy* (1504) where he also decorated the cupboards. The beautiful *candelabrum* of carved wood and the *lectern* which stand in the Choir are also by Fra Giovanni. The frescoes in the sacristy depicting *Popes and Benedictine Monks* are by Domenico and Francesco Morone. The *Landscapes* and the lower portions of the wall cupboards are by D. Brusasorci. The altarpiece depicting *Saints Anthony and Francis* is by Orbetto. In a room near the Sacristy is a XIIIth Cent. wooden sculpture of *Christ riding on a Mule.*

LEFT AISLE. – Fourth chapel, *Madonna and Saints* by Savoldo. Third chapel, *Madonna with Saints Augustine and Zeno*, F. Morone, 1503.

THE LOWER CHURCH. – This is a particularly interesting example of early Romanesque Veronese architecture. It has a nave and two aisles. An important XIVth Cent. marble polyptych depicting *Madonna and Saints* is on the altar in the apse.

The church of San Giovanni in Valle.

CHURCH OF SAN GIOVANNI IN VALLE

(In Via San Giovanni in Valle). This very ancient church was rebuilt after the earthquake of 1117, and was again badly damaged during the last war. It has a nave, two aisles and three apses, and is built entirely of stone. It was of fundamental importance in the development of the Veronese Romanesque style, and many similar churches were modelled on it.

THE FAÇADE. – Severe and simple, it has side windows and a central mullioned window. The XVth Cent. portal is of marble, covered by a porch. In the lunette is an important fresco by Stefano da Verona, depicting the *Madonna and Saints*. The belltower is Romanesque, with an upper section added in the XVIIIth Cent. The remains of the cloister, along the right hand side of the church, are Romanesque like the tombstones.

THE INTERIOR possesses a very pronounced atmosphere, with a narrow central nave in striking contrast with the wider side-aisles from which it is divided by a series of pillars and columns with Corinthian capitals. The ceiling is supported by wooden cross-beams. A XVIIth Cent. staircase leads up to the raised presbytery.

THE CRYPT is reached from the presbytery, and has three aisles as well and contains many traces of the original church. There are two rare examples of Early Christian sculpture – both *Sarcophagi*. The first, of Saints Jude and Taddeus, bears fine reliefs on the sides, and a lid added in 1395. The second, probably of Roman origin, has fluted sides, and niches containing the figures of a husband and wife, with *Saints Peter and Paul* on the sides.

Panorama of the Roman Theatre; below: ***entrance to the theatre.***

THE ROMAN THEATRE

This Roman Theatre, which is superbly positioned on the banks of the river Adige, was built in the second half of the Ist Cent. B.C. Successive construction caused the theatre to disappear. The excavations which brought it to light were commenced by the archeologist Andrea Monga in the middle of the XIXth Cent. and were only finished comparatively recently. The theatre contains semicircular tiers of seats, partly rebuilt. The stage, which has only been partly recovered, is flanked by the impressive ruins of the wings. Unfortunately, very little remains of the imposing façade which once faced the river Adige. Set against the green tufa hills, crowned by the ancient Monastery of St. Jerome, the theatre is very impressive. Above the last tier of seats to the left is a loggia with marble columns which once formed part of the theatre, though it seems unlikely that this was its original position. An unusual feature is the wide, deep trench dug into the tufa behind the Theatre to separate it from the mountain side.

Ponte Pietra seen from the Roman Theatre; entrance to the theater. Next page: *tiers in the Roman Theatre and the church of Saints Sirus and Libera.*

THE CHURCH OF SAINTS SIRUS AND LIBERA

The church stands on the eastern side of the theatre and is theonly remaining building of the many which were built on this site over the years. It was founded in the time of Berengarius in the Xth Cent. and was changed considerably over the centuries, especially in the XVIIth Cent. A double Baroque staircase leads up to the church, but the *façade* still preserves its XIVth Cent. door and porch, and the contemporary statue of *Saint Libera* in the lunette. The church possesses many interesting items, including: a XVIIIth Cent. *Madonna and St. Gaetano* by Giambettino Cignaroli, in the first chapel on the left. The very fine *High Altar* decorated with inlaid marble panels and statues. The splendid *choir stalls* by three Germans: Kraft, Petendorf and Siut (1717-1720). There is also a painting of the *Annunciation* by Ridolfi, and a *Bust of Pope Clement XIII* above the door.

A room in the Archaeological Museum; below: ***mosaic of gladiators in combat, 1st Cen. A.D.***

THE ARCHAEOLOGICAL MUSEUM

Access to this museum is by lift from the Roman Theatre (ask the Custodian). The museum occupies part of what was once the Monastery of St. Jerome. It offers the visitor a fund of information essential to an understanding of Verona in Roman times.

ROOM 1 (The New Room). – Important mosaics among which outstanding scenes of gladiatorial combat dating from the Ist Cent. A.D. The sculptures include the *Head of a Prince of the Julio-Claudian Family*, and a *Bust of a Man in Armour*, both dating from the Ist Cent. The glass showcases contain a fine collection of ceramics produced both in Greece itself, and by the Greeks who colonised Italy before the Romans.

ROOM II, III and IV (Monks' cells). – Sculpture, bronzes, glass etc. The bronzes include a *statuette of Tiberius*, a portrait of the Augustan era, and a double faced *Head of Hermes*.

CORRIDOR. – Roman sculpture, the most important of which is a statue of *Menander*, a Roman copy of a Greek original dating from the IIIrd Cent. B.C.

Bronze portrait from the Augustan era; bust of a Man in Armour Roman period; below: *a room on the Archaeological Museum.*

REFECTORY. – Contains sculpture, urns from Volterra, inscribed gravestones, and mosaics. Outstanding among the sculptures is a *Seated Female Figure*. This is a Roman IInd Cent. copy of the Venus of the Garden, a Greek

Venus of the Garden; below: *Room of the Inscriptions.*

Above: ***satyr;*** below: ***double-faced Hermes.***

statue of the period of Phidias. Also of note are a *Statue of a Man*, which is a Roman copy of a IVth Cent. Greek statue, and a *Zeus*, also copied from a Greek original.

COURTYARD AND CLOISTER OF St. JEROME. – Roman sarcophagi and Veronese tombs.

CHURCH OF St. JEROME. – An early Christian pavement from St. Stephen is preserved here. The triumphal arch is decorated with a fresco by Fr. Caroto. *The Annunciation* (1508), and a XVth Cent. triptych above the altar. To the right of the altar is a rare and extremely interesting IVth Cent. statue of the *Good Shepherd*.

THE SECOND CLOISTER. – This was severely damaged in the XVIIIth Cent. Some small fragments of sarcophagi are preserved here, together with a IInd Cent. *double faced Hermes*, a *Head of Heracles*, and others. Finally, there is a most interesting chamber, the *Nymphaion*, a part of the Roman building which probably once had some connection with the Theatre below. Beautiful view over the town.

Cloister of St. Jerome; below: *church of Saint Jerome.*

PONTE PIETRA

Verona had two bridges in Roman times, and this one, which was formerly known as the *Pons Marmoreus*, is the only one that remains. Fragments of the other one, known as the *Postumio*, are visible on the banks of the river near the Church of St. Anastasia. Ponte Pietra dates from the Pre-Augustan period, and has five arches. The arch next to the right hand bank was rebuilt in 1298, together with the tall watch tower, by Alberto della Scala. The contrast between the materials used in the building and the reconstruction, makes this bridge very picturesque. Most of the four arches on the left, and some of the piers were destroyed at the end of the Second World War, in April 1945.

Watchtower on the Ponte Pietra; below and next page: *two views of the ponte Pietra.*

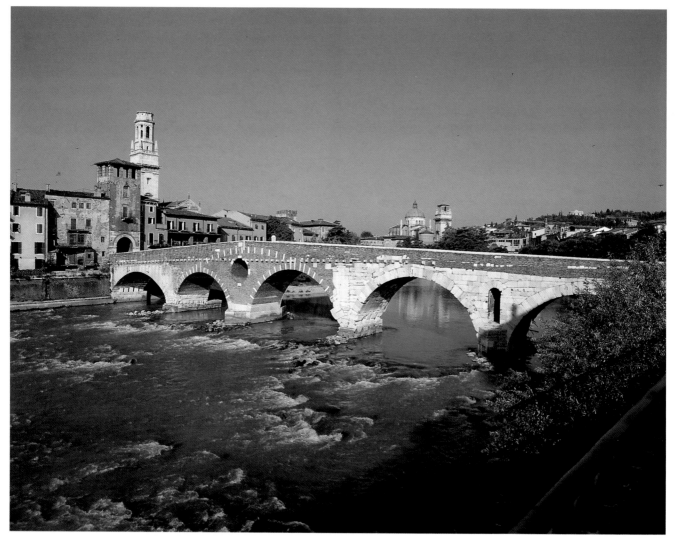

The church of Santo Stefano.

SANTO STEFANO

(Piazza Santo Stefano). – A tradition exists in Verona that this church, a masterpiece of Veronese Romanesque architecture, was intended to be the city's first Cathedral. An oratory existed on the site as early as the VIth Cent., but it was destroyed by Theodoric and rebuilt in the VIIIth Cent. The present building, however, was founded in the XIIth Cent. and the apse is the result of XIVth Cent. alterations. The traditional stone and brick decoration on the *Façade*, together with the elegant stone pillars and the hanging porch above the entrance give the church a very fine appearance. An unusual aspect of the exterior is the robust octagonal drum above the cross-vault.

THE INTERIOR. – Typical basilica design with a central nave divided from the aisles by broad pillars, and a raised presbytery section.

THE RIGHT SIDE. – The *Chapel of the Innocents* (1619-1621) is decorated in exotic Baroque style with frescoes by Ottino depicting *The Assumption* and *the Virtues*. *The Slaughter of the Innocents* above the altar is also by Ottino. To the right is an important work by the most famous of all Veronese XVIIth Cent. painters, Marcanto-nio Bassetti, showing the *Five Bishops of Verona*, to whom the chapel is dedicated. Facing it is the *Forty Martyrs* by Orbetto. In the lunette above the side door the fresco with *Saint Stephen and the Holy Innocents* is by B. Dal Moro.

THE PRESBYTERY. – This is the most important part of the church, and its outstanding feature is a rare *semicircular gallery*, the columns which support it bearing capitals from the original VIIIth Cent. church. There is also a contemporary *Bishop's Throne* (or "Cathedra"), which gave rise to the legend of this church's Cathedral status. The cupola is decorated with frescoes by Domenico Brusasorci (1523), and on the right side of the Presbytery is *The Madonna with Saints Peter and Paul* by Fr. Caroto. The left hand chapel contains the frescoed *The Annunciation* and *The Coronation of the Virgin Mary*, attributed to the School of Stefano da Verona.

THE CRYPT. – Several elements of the early building survive here, particularly the ancient capitals on the pillars, and fragments of XIIIth Cent. frescoes, whereas the statue of St. Peter is XIVth Cent.

SAN GIORGIO IN BRAIDA

This church was founded in 1447 and designed by Antonio Ricci. It was built on the site of a small VIIIth Cent. church, dedicated to the same saint. Around the middle of the XVIth Cent. the drum and the cupola were designed by Sanmicheli. He was also responsible for the belltower, which was never finished.

The façade is XVIIth Cent. French shot spattered the house next door in 1805. The damage is still visible.

THE INTERIOR. – The church, as well as being one of the richest in works of art in Verona, is also outstanding for the excellence of its design. It has one central nave, with side chapels opening off it. On the wall above the main door *The Baptism of Christ*, by Jacopo Tintoretto. At the beginning of the nave two remarkable XVIth Cent. holy water stoups, with statues of St. John the Baptist and St. George.

First chapel on the right. *Christ and Mary Magdalene* by Fr. Montemezzano XVIth Cent. Second chapel on the right. *The Assumption of the Virgin Mary* by P. Ottino. Third chapel on the right. *Pentecost* by Domenico Tintoretto. Fourth chapel on the right. *The Virgin Mary and Archangels*, by Domenico Brusasorci.

At each side of the Choir the two sections of a painting by Romanino *The Judgement of St. George* (XVIth Cent.).

THE PRESBYTERY. – On the balustrade are *statues of the Apostles* in bronze, stylistically similar to those on the holy water stoups. To one side of the Presbytery is *The Announcing Angel*, and this is balanced on the other side by *The Virgin Mary*, both by Fr. Caroto. Behind the altar hangs one of the finest works by Paolo Veronese: *The Martyrdom of Saint George*, painted between 1565 and 1566. On each side of the XVIth Cent. organ is another work by Romanino in two parts – *The Martyrdom of Saint George*.

Fourth chapel on the left. One of the major works of Girolamo dai Libri, *Madonna with Saints Zeno and Lorenzo Giustiniani, with Angelic Musicians*. Third chapel on the left. A *Triptych*, which includes *The Transfiguration* by Francesco Caroto; the lunette is by Domenico Brusasorci. Second chapel on the left, *Martyrdom of Saint Laurence* by Sigism. De Stefani (1564). First chapel on the left, *Saint Ursula and the Virgins* by F. Caroto.

The church of San Giorgio in Braida.

View of the Castel San Pietro.

THE RIVER ADIGE, THE HILLS AND VIEWPOINTS

The River *Adige* winds through the heart of Verona, and is one of the salient features of its landscape. The river enters the city on high ground, at the Chievo Dam, and it is here that the bridges begin. The first is the recently built *Ponte del Saval*, then the *Ponte Catena*, which is modern; then comes the *Ponte del Risorgimento*, designed by P.L. Nervi, 1966-1968; *Ponte del Castelvecchio* (1355); *Ponte della Vittoria*, by the architect E. Fagiuoli, a postwar reconstruction; *Ponte Garibaldi*; *Ponte Pietra* (Roman); *Ponte Nuovo*; *Ponte delle Navi*; *Ponte Aleardi*, by the architect M. Zamarchi; *Ponte San Francesco*; and finally *Ponte della Ferrovia*, built by the Austrians in the XIXth Cent.

The *Hills of Verona*, which provide a picturesque backdrop to the city, rise in a semicircle to the North East, and have a beneficial influence on the climate.

The hills are now being cared for after the long years of neglect to which foreign domination had consigned them. The network of roads is being repaired and expanded. There is a reafforestation programme, and residential areas, sportsgrounds and public open spaces are being developed. From these gentle hills there are many *good vantage points* from which one can enjoy beautiful views over the town in the valley. The best of these are the new road, the *Strada dei Colli*, the belvedere in front of the *Sanctuary of St. Leonard*, *Piazza of the Castel San Pietro*, and the road known as the *Strada delle Torricelle*. Outstanding views of the city are often obtainable from the various bridges over the River Adige, particularly from the Ponte del Castelvecchio, Ponte Garibaldi, Ponte Pietra, Ponte Nuovo and Ponte delle Navi.

Two panoramic views.